Golf!

GREAT
MOMENTS
&
DUBIOUS
ACHIEVEMENTS
IN GOLF
HISTORY

•

FLOYD CONNER

•

CHRONICLE BOOKS

SAN FRANCISCO

Printed in Singapore.

ISBN 0-8118-0128-4

Library of Congress Cataloging in Publication Data available.

Distributed in Canada by Raincoast Books, 112 East Third Avenue, Vancouver, B.C. V5T 1C8

10 9 8 7 6 5 4

Chronicle Books
275 Fifth Street
San Francisco, CA 94103

Introduction

Ever since the Royal Scottish Archers abandoned their posts 500 years ago in order to practice their drives and chip shots, people have been obsessed with golf. The game moved to the United States in 1888, when John Reid converted a cow pasture in Yonkers, New York, into the nation's first golf course. And in 1971, golf became the first sport to be played on the moon, where Alan Shepard picked up a 6-iron and hit a ball for miles.

Today, millions of players heft their bags every week and set out for the excitement, frustration, exercise, relaxation, and camaraderie of a round of golf. Millions more watch the Masters, PGA, British Open, and other televised championships, waiting in silent concentration as pros line up putts that may win or lose hundreds of thousands of dollars.

Golf has become a passion that is shared by amateurs and professionals, men and women, young and old. Part of its allure is that it remains one of the most unpredictable of sports: duffers sometimes score a hole-in-one, while exalted players are humbled by a single errant shot.

Golf! Great Moments & Dubious Achievements presents the triumphant and embarrassing stories behind more than 200 one-of-a-kind golfing feats of the past century. Each player has the distinction of being *the only golfer* to perform these remarkable exploits.

Of course there are the legendary accomplishments of the great golfers: Bobby Jones was the only golfer to win the Grand Slam, Byron Nelson the only one to win 11 consecutive professional tournaments. But there are many more entries devoted to the most thrilling feat in golf, the hole-in-one. In fact, most hole-in-one records are held by little-known golfers: Larry Bruce has the longest (480 yards) and Scott Palmer the most (100).

Golf can be inspiring: Charles Boswell, blinded during World War II, subsequently shot a round of 81. Golf can also be dangerous: Bayly MacArthur nearly perished when he hit his ball into a quicksand trap, and Jack Nicklaus and Gary Player were attacked by a swarm of killer bees.

The sport has its trying moments, too: A. J. Lewis putted 156 times on one green and still did not hole out, and Sam Snead is the only player to lose a tournament because he hit into the men's restroom.

So what follows is a truly unique collection of official records and bizarre—but documented—nineteenth hole stories. Whatever your handicap, wherever you play, and however unusual you think your experiences are, you will be amazed at the ways each of these players drove, putted, and shanked their way to golf immortality.

Margaret Abbott

THE ONLY WOMAN GOLFER to win an Olympic gold medal.

Golf was introduced as an Olympic sport at the 1900 Olympics in Paris. Women golfers from the United States and France competed in the 9-hole event. American Margaret Abbott shot a 47 to win the gold medal by two shots. Some of the French women had never played golf and wore high heels and tight skirts. Women's golf was discontinued in the Olympics after 1900.

Spiro Agnew

THE ONLY GOLFER to hit three spectators with his first two tee shots in a tournament.

Vice President Spiro Agnew was invited to play in the Pro-Am portion of the 1971 Bob Hope Desert Classic in Palm Springs, California. After hitting three spectators with his first two tee shots, Agnew decided, in the interest of public safety, to put his clubs away for the day.

Ray Ainsley

THE ONLY GOLFER to shoot a triple triple triple triple bogey in the US Open.

For a professional golfer, a triple bogey is a disaster. On June 10, 1938, Ray Ainsley made a triple triple triple triple bogey during the US Open played at the Cherry Hills Country Club in Englewood, Colorado. Ainsley hit a ball into a creek and took 13 shots to hit it out. By the time he finished, he was 12 shots over par for the hole.

Dr. Alcorn

THE ONLY GOLFER to score a double birdie.

Dr. Alcorn of Wentworth Falls, Australia, was playing the 9th hole of the Leura Golf Club in Wentworth in 1928. He hit his second shot just as a player on the other side of the fairway hit his approach shot. The two balls collided in midair and both fell into the cup for the only double birdie in golf history.

Amy Alcott

THE ONLY GOLFER to shoot 280 in the US Women's Open.

Amy Alcott set the record for the lowest score in the history of the US Women's Open when she shot 280 in 1980. Alcott had her best year on the LPGA Tour in 1980, winning four tournaments.

C. H. Alison

THE ONLY GOLFER to hit a shot from the roof of the clubhouse.

In 1904 C. H. Alison was on the final hole of a close match when he hit his approach shot onto the roof of the clubhouse at Woking Golf Course in England. Rather than concede the hole, he climbed a ladder and played the shot. He hit a miraculous shot on the green and halved the hole.

Willie Anderson

THE ONLY GOLFER to win three consecutive US Opens.

Only one player has won three consecutive US Open Championships. Willie Anderson won the Open in 1903, 1904, and 1905. He also won the title in 1901, giving him four championships in five years.

George Archer

ONE OF THE ONLY GOLFERS to use fewer than 95 putts during a 72-hole tournament.

The greatest display of putting in a tournament belonged to George Archer. At the 1980 Sea Pines Heritage Classic at Harbour Town Golf Course on Hilton Head Island in South Carolina, Archer required only 94 putts during the 72-hole tournament. The figure was 5 under the PGA tournament record.

Tommy Armour

THE ONLY ONE-EYED GOLFER to win the US Open.

Tommy Armour lost an eye in World War I but overcame the handicap to become a champion golfer. Armour won the US Open in 1927, earning the first of his three major titles. In 1930 Armour won the PGA Championship and the following year the British Open.

Michael Austin

THE ONLY GOLFER to drive a ball 515 yards in tournament play.

Sixty-four-year-old Michael Austin accomplished a feat no other golfer has ever matched when he drove a golf ball 515 yards during the United States National Seniors' Championship in Las Vegas, Nevada, on September 25, 1974. Aided by a 35-mile-per-hour tail wind, the 210-pound Los Angeles native drove the ball within a yard of the 450-yard hole. The momentum was so great that it carried the shot 65 yards past the stick. The mammoth drive took place on the fifth hole of the Winterwood Golf Course.

David Ayton

THE ONLY GOLFER to blow a five-shot lead with two holes to play in the British Open.

David Ayton appeared to be a sure winner when he came to the 17th hole of the 1885 British Open with a five-shot lead. Ayton scored an 11 on St. Andrews's notorious Road Hole and lost the tournament by two shots.

John Ball

THE ONLY GOLFER to use a black ball to win a bet.

One day in 1907, a dense fog rolled over the Hoylake Golf Course in Cheshire, England, making play almost impossible. Someone bet champion golfer John Ball that he could not play a round under 90 without losing a ball. He accepted the bet and shot an 81 without losing a single ball. His secret was that he used a black ball for better visibility in the fog.

Seve Ballesteros

THE ONLY GOLFER to win the Masters at age 23.

Seve Ballesteros of Spain was the dominant international player of the 1980s. In 1979, at the age of 22, he won his first British Open title. The following year, the 23-year-old Spaniard became the youngest player ever to win the Masters, posting a winning score of 13 under par 275. Three years later Ballesteros added a second Masters title.

Laura Baugh

THE ONLY GOLFER to win the US Women's Amateur title at age 16.

In 1971, at age 16, Laura Baugh became the youngest golfer to win the US Women's Amateur Championship. The victory launched a highly successful professional career in which Baugh became one of the most popular players on the LPGA tour.

Andy Bean

THE ONLY GOLFER to lose a tournament by making a putt.

Andy Bean once lost the 1983 Canadian Open by making a putt. In the third round he sank a two-inch putt using the grip of the putter, a violation of the rules for which he was penalized two shots. The following day he scored a sensational 62 but lost the tournament by two shots.

Patty Berg

THE ONLY WOMAN GOLFER to win 16 major tournaments.

Patty Berg holds the all-time record for major tournament victories by a woman. She won seven Titleholders Championships, seven Western Opens, one US Open, and one US Women's Amateur for a total of 16 major titles. Mickey Wright and Louise Suggs are next on the list with 13 major titles.

Richard Blackman

THE ONLY GOLFER to be chased off a golf course by a lion.

Richard Blackman and his partner, William Smithline, were playing the 16th hole of the Paradise Island Golf Course in Nassau, Bahamas, when they were confronted by a lion. The two golfers fled for their lives, and the lion, which had escaped from a circus, was captured.

Homero Blancas

THE ONLY GOLFER to shoot a round of 55 in a professional tournament.

The record for the lowest round in a professional tournament was set by Homero Blancas. On August 19, 1962, he shot 55 in the first round of the Premier Invitational Tournament held in Longview, Texas.

Tommy Bolt

THE ONLY GOLFER to be fined for passing gas.

Tommy Bolt was known for his uncontrollable temper and he was no stranger to fines. At the 1959 Memphis Invitational Open, Bolt was assessed one of the strangest fines in PGA tour history. His playing partner was about to putt when Bolt loudly passed gas. Officials were not amused and fined him $250 for unsportsmanlike behavior.

Julius Boros

THE ONLY GOLFER to win a Grand Slam tournament at age 48.

Julius Boros was an accountant who did not turn professional until he was 30 years old. In 1963, at the age of 43, he won the US Open in a play-off with Arnold Palmer and Jackie Cupit. Five years later he won the PGA title, making him the oldest player ever to win a Grand Slam event.

Charles Boswell

THE ONLY BLIND GOLFER to shoot a round of 81.

Charles Boswell of Birmingham, Alabama, never played golf before he was blinded by shellfire during World War II. After his injury he became an expert golfer, once shooting a round of 81.

Ollie Bowersof

THE ONLY GOLFER to play over 10,000 holes of golf in one year.

Ollie Bowersof of Gafney, South Carolina, played more golf in a year than most people play in a lifetime. He played 10,075 holes in one year, the equivalent of 560 rounds of golf.

Mathieu Boya

THE ONLY GOLFER to hit a drive that destroyed a country's entire air force.

Mathieu Boya was the most avid golfer in Benin. The only problem was that the small African country did not have a golf course. Boya practiced hitting golf balls in an open field next to the Benin Air Base. In 1987 one of his drives struck a bird flying over the base. The stunned bird fell into the open cockpit of a fighter jet about to take off. The pilot lost control of the plane and crashed into four Mirage jets, the entire Benin Air Force, parked on the runway. All five planes, worth over $40 million, were destroyed.

Joseph Boydstone

THE ONLY GOLFER to score three holes-in-one on the front 9.

Joseph Boydstone, the only golfer to score three holes-in-one on the front 9 of a round, performed the unique feat on the 3rd, 4th, and 9th holes of the Bakersfield Golf Club course in Bakersfield, California, on October 10, 1962.

Harry Bradshaw

THE ONLY GOLFER to lose the British Open because of a beer bottle.

Harry Bradshaw was one stroke behind the leader in the 1949 British Open when he teed off on the 451 yard, par-4 fifth hole at Royal St. George's in Sandwich, England. His drive landed atop a broken beer bottle in the rough. Bradshaw elected to play the ball where it lay. His shot traveled only 25 yards and he took a double bogey 6 on the hole. He later lost the Open in a play-off with Bobby Locke.

R. W. Bridges

THE ONLY GOLFER to score a hole-in-one with his putter.

In 1931 R. W. Bridges decided to use a putter when he teed off on a 196-yard hole at the Woodlawn Country Club in Kirkwood, Missouri. The result was the longest putt in golf history, a 196-yard hole-in-one.

Mary Brown

THE ONLY GOLFER to be given a second chance to putt in a tournament.

Mary Brown was on the 18th green during the Southern California Women's Open when a sudden downpour briefly halted play. When play resumed, she attempted to putt out. The cup was filled with water, and when she putted, the ball floated right over the hole. Tournament officials decided that she had been unfairly victimized on the hole and allowed her to putt a second time after the cup was drained.

Larry Bruce

THE ONLY GOLFER to score a hole-in-one on a 480-yard dogleg hole.

In the long history of golf, no player has ever hit a longer hole-in-one than Larry Bruce. On November 15, 1962, Bruce was playing the 480-yard fifth hole at the Hope Country Club in Hope, Arkansas. Bruce decided to shorten the distance to the hole by hitting the ball through the dogleg. The strategy paid off as he aced the hole.

Otto Bucher

THE ONLY GOLFER to score a hole-in-one at age 99.

Just four months shy of his 100th birthday, Otto Bucher became the oldest golfer to score a hole-in-one. The Swiss golfer aced the 130-yard 12th hole at the La Manga Golf Course in Spain on January 13, 1985.

Billy Burke

THE ONLY GOLFER to win the US Open in a 72-hole play-off.

Billy Burke and George Von Elm were tied after 72 holes in the 1931 US Open, played at the Inverness Country Club in Toledo, Ohio. They were still tied after a 36-hole play-off. Burke and Von Elm were forced to play another 36 holes. Burke won by one stroke, 148 to 149.

Bernard Burkett

THE ONLY GOLFER to score holes-in-one in five different decades.

Bernard Burkett spread his six holes-in-one over five different decades. He had holes-in-one in 1937, 1950, 1958, 1961, 1971, and 1980.

Mark Calcavecchia

THE ONLY PROFESSIONAL GOLFER forced to withdraw from a tournament for being dirty.

Mark Calcavecchia was playing the sixth hole of the 1986 Kemper Open at the TPC-Avenel Course in Potomac, Maryland, when he drove the ball into a ravine. As he climbed down the hill to reach his ball, he slid into a mud puddle. His clothes were covered with mud and he withdrew from the tournament a few holes later.

Dorothy Campbell

THE ONLY GOLFER to win 750 tournaments.

Dorothy Campbell was the most successful woman golfer at the turn of the century. The Scot won the amateur championships of the United States, Great Britain, and Canada. During her career she won an unprecedented 750 tournaments worldwide.

Al Capone

THE ONLY GOLFER to shoot himself while playing golf.

Al Capone was a better gangster than a golfer. In 1928 he was playing golf at the Burnham Woods Golf Course near Chicago, when a gun he kept in his golf bag for protection accidentally went off, wounding Scarface in the foot.

Bill Carey

THE ONLY GOLFER to lose a hole while shooting a hole-in-one.

It seems impossible to lose a hole by shooting a hole-in-one but Bill Carey did just that. On an evening in July 1964, Carey was playing a match with Edgar Winter at the Roehampton Golf Course in England. The sun was about to set as Carey and Winter played the seventh hole. Winter's shot landed close to the pin but they could not find Carey's ball in the darkness. Only after he conceded the hole did he discover that his ball was in the bottom of the cup and that he had made a hole-in-one.

JoAnne Carner

THE ONLY GOLFER to win an LPGA tournament at age 46.

JoAnne Carner won five US Women's Amateur Championships before turning professional. The late start did not stop Carner from winning over 40 professional tournaments. In 1985 the 46-year-old Carner won the Safeco Classic to become the oldest player to win an LPGA tournament.

James Carvill

THE ONLY GOLFER to play an 18-hole round of golf in just over 27 minutes.

Twenty-one-year-old James Carvill holds the distinction of playing the fastest round of golf in history. On June 18, 1987, Carvill completed 18 holes at the Warrenpoint Golf Club course in Down, Ireland, in just 27 minutes, 9 seconds.

Billy Casper

THE ONLY GOLFER to win the US Open after being seven shots down with 9 holes to play.

Arnold Palmer led the 1966 US Open at the Olympic Club in San Francisco by seven shots with only 9 holes to play. Billy Casper staged an amazing comeback and tied Palmer after 72 holes. The stunned Palmer lost the play-off to Casper.

Al Chandler

THE ONLY PROFESSIONAL GOLFER to whiff three times on the same hole.

During the 1986 Senior Tournament Players Championship at the Canterbury Country Club near Cleveland, Ohio, Al Chandler suffered the ignominy of whiffing three times on the 15th hole. On the par-4 hole Chandler hit a shot near an oak tree. He missed the ball twice attempting a chip-in on the green, then, incredibly, whiffed again while attempting a tap-in.

Bob Charles

THE ONLY LEFT-HANDED GOLFER to win the British Open.

Bob Charles is probably the greatest left-handed golfer of all time. In 1963 the native of New Zealand became the only left-handed golfer to win the British Open.

Tze-Chung Chen

THE ONLY GOLFER to score a double eagle in the US Open.

Taiwan's Tze-Chung Chen is the only golfer to score a double eagle (three under par) on a hole in the long history of the US Open. The rare double eagle occurred during the first round of the championship, held at the Oakland Hills Golf Course in Birmingham, Michigan.

Willie Chisholm

THE ONLY GOLFER to score an 18 on a par 3 hole in the US Open.

Willie Chisholm found himself caught between a rock and a hard place at the 1919 US Open. His tee shot on the 185-yard, par 3 eighth hole at the Brae Burn Country Club in West Newton, Massachusetts, lodged against a boulder short of the green. It took Chisholm 13 swings before he could pry the ball loose from its rocky lie. As a result, the Scot took 18 strokes to complete the hole.

Archie Compston

THE ONLY GOLFER to use three caddies at the same time.

Archie Compston, one of the best English golfers of the 1920s, was the only golfer to employ three caddies simultaneously. One caddy carried his clubs. Another was required to carry his golf apparel. The third attended to his smoking needs. The tobacco caddy carried cigarettes, cigars, and pipes for the chainsmoking golfer.

Bob Cook

THE ONLY GOLFER to sink a 140-foot putt during a tournament.

The record for the longest measured holed putt during a tournament belongs to Bob Cook. He rolled in a 140 footer on the finishing hole of the Old St. Andrews course in Fife, Scotland, during the International Fourball Pro-Am Tournament on October 1, 1976.

R. H. Corbett

THE ONLY GOLFER to shoot 9 straight 3s.

At the 1916 Tangye Cup in Mullim, England, R. H. Corbett shot the most consistent 9-hole score in golf history. He scored a 3 on all 9 holes for an 8-under total of 27. Corbett had two eagles, four birdies, and three pars during that span.

Henry Cotton

THE ONLY GOLFER to shoot a 36-hole score of 132 at the British Open.

In 1934 Henry Cotton shot the lowest 36-hole score in British Open history. He dominated Royal St. George's Course in Sandwich, England, with rounds of 67 and 65 to open up a commanding 9-shot lead. Despite a final round 79, he won the tournament by 5 shots.

Ben Crenshaw

THE ONLY GOLFER to be named college player of the year for three straight years.

Ben Crenshaw has had an outstanding professional career, highlighted by a victory in the 1984 Masters. Before he turned professional, he played golf for the University of Texas. Crenshaw was the only player to be voted male collegiate golfer of the year for three consecutive years, from 1971 to 1973.

Fay Crocker

THE ONLY GOLFER to win the US Women's Open at age 40.

Life began at 40 for golfer Fay Crocker. The native of Uruguay was a month short of her 41st birthday when she won the 1955 US Open, becoming the oldest winner in the tournament's history.

Bobby Cruickshank

THE ONLY GOLFER to lose the US Open because he knocked himself out with his own
club.

Bobby Cruickshank was leading the
1934 US Open played at the Merion Golf
Course in Philadelphia when he hit a
miraculous shot on the 11th hole. The ball
skipped across a water hazard and came to
rest safely on the green. In celebration, he
threw his club in the air. The club landed
on his head, knocking him cold. The woozy
Cruickshank relinquished the lead and ul-
timately finished third.

Thad Daber

THE ONLY GOLFER to shoot a round of 70 while using only one club.

Thad Daber of Durham, North Carolina, shot a 2-under-par round of 70 during the 1987 World One Club Championship at Cary, North Carolina. The tournament was played over the 6,037-yard Lochmere Golf Club Course. Each competitor was allowed to select one club to use for the entire round. Daber used a 6-iron during his record-setting round.

Roberto de Vicenzo

THE ONLY GOLFER to lose the Masters because he signed an incorrect scorecard.

Roberto de Vicenzo won over 200 tournaments around the world but he is best remembered for one he lost. He finished the 1968 Masters tied for first with Bob Goalby. De Vicenzo did not notice that his playing partner, Tommy Aaron, had mistakenly added a stroke to his scorecard. When de Vicenzo signed the incorrect scorecard, he was forced to accept the score—and second place.

Judy Dickinson

THE ONLY WOMAN GOLFER to shoot a 36-hole score under 130.

The lowest 36-hole score in an LPGA tournament was turned in by Judy Dickinson at the 1985 S & H Golf Classic held at the Pasadena Yacht and Country Club in Florida. She shot rounds of 64 and 65 for a two-day total of 129.

Bob Dickson

THE ONLY GOLFER to be penalized four shots for having another golfer's club in his bag.

While playing in the 1965 US Amateur Championship, Bob Dickson noticed that he had 15 clubs in his bag, one over the acceptable limit. He notified officials and was penalized four shots. Ironically, the club belonged to another golfer who had put it in Dickson's bag by mistake.

Helen Dobson

THE ONLY GOLFER to drive a golf ball more than 530 yards during a round of golf.

Driving a golf ball is more a matter of timing than of pure brute strength. The record for driving a golf ball under normal conditions is by Helen Dobson. She hit the historic 531-yard shot at RAF Honington, England, on October 31, 1987.

Charlotte Dod

THE ONLY GOLFER to win both Wimbledon and the Ladies' British Open.

Charlotte Dod was a champion in two sports. In 1887 she won her first Wimbledon tennis championship at the age of 15. Between 1887 and 1893 she won five Wimbledon singles titles. Turning her attention to golf, she won the Ladies' British Open in 1904.

Catherine Duggan

THE ONLY GOLFER to complete an LPGA
tournament round in 95 minutes.

Catherine Duggan played the fastest
round in LPGA history during the 1984
Sarasota Classic in Florida. Duggan and
her playing partner, Lynn Adams, toured
the Bent Tree Golf and Racquet Club
course in just 1 hour and 35 minutes.
Duggan shot 72 while Adams struggled in
with a round of 78.

George Duncan

THE ONLY GOLFER to win the British Open after being 13 shots behind after two rounds.

George Duncan was 13 shots behind leader Abe Mitchell at the midway point of the 1920 British Open played at Deal in England. Duncan made up 13 shots in one round as he fired a 71, while Mitchell ballooned to an 84. Duncan capped off his comeback with a two-shot victory the following day.

Denis Durnian

THE ONLY GOLFER to shoot 28 for 9 holes at
the British Open.

Denis Durnian owns the 9-hole record at
the British Open. He shot a 28 during the
second round of the 1983 British Open
played at the Royal Birkdale course in
Southport, England.

Chick Evans, Jr.

THE ONLY GOLFER to play in 50 consecutive US Amateur Championships.

Chick Evans, Jr., set a longevity record by playing in 50 consecutive US Amateur Championships. In 1916 he won both the US Amateur and US Open championships. The great Bobby Jones was the only other golfer to win both championships in the same year. Evans won his first US Amateur Championship in 1907.

Paul Farmer

THE ONLY PROFESSIONAL GOLFER to receive 18 penalty strokes during a round.

Paul Farmer was in contention during the third round of the 1960 Texas Open until he decided to change putters. He had just finished the 9th hole of the Fort Sam Houston Golf Course in San Antonio, Texas, when he elected to use another putter for the back 9. After completing the round, he learned that he had been penalized two strokes per hole for changing putters. Under the rules he could only change putters if the club was broken. The 18 penalty strokes ballooned his day's score to 88.

Vicki Fergon

THE ONLY GOLFER to make 11 birdies in
one round of an LPGA tournament.

Vicki Fergon burned up the Almaden
Golf and Country Club Course during the
second round of the 1984 San Jose Classic
in San Jose, California. She made an LPGA
record 11 birdies while shooting a round
of 62.

Raymond Floyd

THE ONLY PROFESSIONAL GOLFER to hit a drive into his own golf bag.

During his career Raymond Floyd has won the US Open, Masters, and PGA championships. One of his least memorable moments occurred in the first round of the 1987 Tournament Players Championship held in Ponte Vedra Beach, Florida. On the 11th hole Floyd hit a good drive over 250 yards down the fairway. He was unaware that his caddy had left his bag lying on the grass. His drive sailed into the golf bag, costing Floyd two penalty shots.

Joe Flynn

THE ONLY GOLFER to throw a ball around a golf course in 82 shots.

A lot of golfers can shoot 82 but Joe Flynn is the only one who has done it by throwing the ball. On March 27, 1975, the 21-year-old Flynn needed just 82 shots to throw a golf ball around the Port Royal Golf Course in Bermuda.

Wayne Grady

THE ONLY GOLFER to be disqualified twice in the same year for hitting the wrong ball.

Wayne Grady was disqualified twice in the same year for hitting someone else's ball. The infractions meant that Grady made early departures from both the 1986 Phoenix Open and the 1986 Los Angeles Open.

P. M. Gregor

THE ONLY GOLFER to win a match because of a grasshopper.

In 1921 P. M. Gregor of Kirkfield, Ontario, Canada, needed to make a long putt to win a match. His putt rolled to the lip of the cup and stopped. Gregor was about to putt it in when a grasshopper landed on the ball. The weight of the grasshopper was enough to knock the ball into the cup, and Gregor won the match.

Oscar Grimes

THE ONLY GOLFER to have a shot land in a cash register.

At the 1939 Western Open qualifier, Oscar Grimes hit a drive that would make a trick-shot artist envious. His wild shot flew into a hamburger stand, landed on the cash register, and fell into the open drawer.

Otis Guernsey

THE ONLY GOLFER to hit a shot that landed on a different golf course in another city.

Otis Guernsey was teeing off at the 9th hole of the Apawanis Golf Club in Rye, New York, when the unexpected happened. He shanked his tee shot onto the 11th green of the adjoining Green Meadows Golf Course. He had hit his shot not only onto another golf course but also into another city. Green Meadows Golf Course lies within the city limits of Harrison, New York.

Jim Hadderer

THE ONLY GOLFER to shoot a hole-in-one on his knees.

In 1965 Jim Hadderer of Elgin, Illinois, scored a hole-in-one on a 190-yard hole at the Wing Park Golf Course in Elgin. What makes the shot even more exceptional was that he hit the drive while on his knees. Hadderer was 16 years old at the time.

Walter Hagen

THE ONLY GOLFER to win four consecutive PGA tournaments.

The great Walter Hagen won 11 major titles during his career. In 1927 he won the PGA Championship held at Cedar Crest Country Club in Dallas, Texas. It was his fourth consecutive PGA title, a record.

Marlene Hagge

THE ONLY GOLFER to win an LPGA tournament at age 18.

Eighteen-year-old Marlene Hagge became the youngest woman ever to win an
LPGA tournament when she captured the
1952 Sarasota Open in Florida. She had a
long and distinguished professional career,
highlighted by a victory in the 1956 LPGA
Championship.

Dick Hardison

THE ONLY GOLFER to shoot a round of 68 in under 50 minutes.

Sixty-one-year-old Dick Hardison took only 49 minutes to shoot a round of 68 at the Sea Mountain Golf Course in Punaluu, Hawaii, on July 21, 1984. He shot a 30 on the back 9 in just 24 minutes.

G. C. Hazen

THE ONLY GOLFER to shoot a magpie-in-one.

Most golfers have shot birdies, some golfers have shot eagles, but G. C. Hazen is the only golfer to shoot a magpie. He teed off at the 105-yard second hole at Daylesford, Australia. His shot struck a tree and ricocheted onto the green where it struck a magpie and rolled into the cup for one of the strangest holes-in-one on record.

Clayton Heafner

THE ONLY PROFESSIONAL GOLFER to withdraw from a tournament because his name was mispronounced.

Clayton Heafner was a fiery competitor, golf's equivalent of Ty Cobb. Just before Heafner was to tee off for the 1941 Oakland Open in Oakland, California, the public address announcer mispronounced his name. Insulted, Heafner stalked off the tee and withdrew from the tournament.

J. M. Heggarty

THE ONLY GOLFER to take four shots from less than a foot away from the pin.

J. M. Heggarty had an easy tap in of less than a foot. Not only did he miss the putt but the ball struck his foot resulting in a two-stroke penalty. He putted out, having taken four shots to make a putt under 12 inches.

Irvin Hemmle

THE ONLY GOLFER to hit over 48,000 practice shots in a year.

If practice makes perfect, then Irvin Hemmle of Fort Worth, Texas, would have been the greatest golfer in the world. In 1983 Hemmle hit 48,265 practice shots, an average of 132 per day.

Sandy Herd

THE ONLY GOLFER to win a non-Seniors tournament at age 58.

Today there is a Senior's Tour for golfers over 50 years old. When 58-year-old Sandy Herd won the 1926 News of the World Match Play Championship, he had to compete against many golfers less than half his age.

Jimmy Hines

THE ONLY GOLFER to score a birdie for his opponent.

Jimmy Hines and Sam Snead were playing partners during a round at the 1938 PGA Championship in Shawnee-on-Delaware, Pennsylvania. Snead was safely on the green when Hines chipped a ball straight at the hole. The shot struck Snead's ball, and both balls rolled into the hole for birdie 2s.

Ben Hogan

THE ONLY GOLFER to win the US Open, British Open, and Masters in the same year.

Ben Hogan made one of the greatest comebacks in sports history. His golf career appeared to be over when he was nearly killed in a head-on collision with a Greyhound bus in 1949. Doctors believed he would never walk again. Hogan amazed the golf world by winning the 1950 US Open. Three years later, he became the only golfer to win the US Open, British Open, and Masters in the same year. He might have won the Grand Slam except that the PGA dates conflicted with those of the British Open.

A. A. Horne

THE ONLY GOLFER to shoot a round of 90 while using a wooden ball.

During World War II, certain materials were in short supply. Some players began using wooden golf balls. A Wooden Ball Championship was held at Potchefstroom, South Africa. A. A. Horne shot a round of 90 to win the tournament.

Bob Hudson

THE ONLY GOLFER to score consecutive
holes-in-one in a tournament.

Bob Hudson made golf history at the
1971 Martini International at Norwich,
England. During the second round, he
aced the 11th and 12th holes, becoming
the only golfer to score back-to-back holes-
in-one in a tournament.

John Humm

THE ONLY GOLFER to shoot a 9-hole score of 34 with one club.

John Humm of Long Island, New York, once played 9 holes of golf using just one club, a 3-iron, and shot 34. The next day he played another 9 using a full set of clubs and shot 40.

William Ingle

THE ONLY GOLFER to begin a round by scoring 1, 2, 3, 4, and 5.

On September 2, 1920, William Ingle aced the first hole of the Torphin Golf Course near Edinburgh, Scotland. He scored a 2 on the second hole, 3 on the third hole, 4 on the fourth hole, and 5 on the fifth hole. If the progression had continued, Ingle would have shot a round of 171.

Hale Irwin

THE ONLY PROFESSIONAL GOLFER to hit a shot into a spectator's bra.

Hale Irwin is one of the best golfers of the past twenty years, winning three US Open Championships. Undoubtedly his most unusual moment occurred in the 1973 Sea Pines Heritage Classic at Hilton Head, South Carolina. One of his shots struck a female spectator in her chest and lodged in her bra. According to the rules, he was instructed to remove the ball from the obstruction and allowed a free drop. Under the circumstances, the woman was permitted to remove the ball herself.

Trish Johnson

THE ONLY WOMAN GOLFER to shoot 242 for a 72-hole tournament.

The lowest 72-hole score ever shot by a woman golfer in a tournament was accomplished by Trish Johnson. She fired a winning score of 242 in the 1987 Eastleigh Classic, held in England.

Bobby Jones

THE ONLY GOLFER to win the Grand Slam.

Bobby Jones was the greatest golfer of his time. During his heyday in the 1920s, he set records that may never be broken. His crowning achievement took place in 1930 when he became the only golfer to win the Grand Slam. In those days the Grand Slam consisted of the US Open, British Open, US Amateur, and British Amateur. Later the amateur tournaments were replaced in the Grand Slam by the Masters and the PGA (US Professional Golfers' Association) Championships. Jones remained an amateur throughout his career and retired at age 28.

Joan Joyce

THE ONLY WOMAN GOLFER to use 17 putts during a round of golf.

Joan Joyce needed only 17 putts in the third round of the 1982 Ladies Michelob Open at the Brookfield West Golf and Country Club in Georgia. She averaged less than one putt per hole in establishing the LPGA record. Before she became a professional golfer, Joyce was the premier women's softball pitcher.

Ralph Kennedy

THE ONLY GOLFER to play on over 3,600 different golf courses.

Ralph Kennedy was the ultimate globe-trotting golfer. Between 1910 and 1953 he played on 3,615 different golf courses. Kennedy played on courses in every state in the US and in 13 foreign countries.

Andrew Kirkaldy

THE ONLY GOLFER to miss a one-inch putt and lose the British Open.

Andrew Kirkaldy lost the 1889 British Open played at Musselburgh, Lothian, Scotland, because he missed a one-inch putt. He whiffed an easy tap in on the 14th hole at Musselburgh Golf Course and finished in a tie with Willie Park, Jr. Park won the 36-hole play-off by five shots.

Joe Kirkwood

THE ONLY GOLFER to use an entire city as a golf course.

After playing a round in the 1928 Tijuana Open, Australian professional Joe Kirkwood bet Walter Hagen $50 he could hit a ball back to the hotel first. The two golfers used the streets of Tijuana for a course. Hagen arrived back at the hotel first but was unable to hit the ball into the toilet, which was designated as a hole. Kirkwood made it on the first try to win the bet.

Robert Klingaman

THE ONLY 58-YEAR-OLD GOLFER to shoot
his age.

The youngest golfer to shoot his age was
Robert Klingaman. On August 31, 1973,
the 58-year-old Klingaman shot a 58 on
the Caledon Golf Club course in
Fayetteville, Pennsylvania.

Kent Kluba

THE ONLY GOLFER to get lost during a tournament.

American Kent Kluba could have used directions during the 1985 French Open. Kluba and his playing partner, Raphael Alarcon, finished the second hole and headed for the third tee. After they teed off, they discovered that the hole they were playing was the thirteenth—not the third. Somehow Kluba and Alarcon had skipped 10 holes.

Bill Kratzert

THE ONLY GOLFER to withdraw from a tournament because he ran out of balls.

On July 11, 1986, Bill Kratzert was playing in the Anheuser Busch Golf Classic in Williamsburg, Virginia. It was a hot summer day, and his caddie did not bring extra balls in order to reduce the weight of the bag he was carrying. Kratzert was having a bad round and lost three balls on errant shots. When he learned that he had run out of golf balls, he was forced to withdraw from the tournament.

Catherine Lacoste

THE ONLY GOLFER to win the US Women's Open at age 22.

Catherine Lacoste of France became the youngest woman to win the US Women's Open. The 22-year-old won the title in 1967, the first amateur to win in over two decades. Her father, Rene Lacoste, was a champion tennis player of the 1920s, winning the US Open, Wimbledon, and the French Open on more than one occasion.

Charlie Law

THE ONLY GOLFER to shoot a round of 75 at age 84.

It is a rarity in golf when a player is able to shoot his or her age. On May 20, 1984, Charlie Law actually shot a score lower than his 84 years. Law shot a round of 75 over the Hayston Course near Glasgow, Scotland.

Harriett O'Brien Lee

THE ONLY GOLFER to make five chip-ins during a round of golf at age 68.

Sixty-eight-year-old Harriett O'Brien Lee was feeling especially chipper during a round of golf at the Meadows Golf Club in Grayeagle, California. She chipped the ball in on five different holes.

Cecilia Leitch

THE ONLY WOMAN GOLFER to win a tournament by 17 holes.

The largest winning margin by a woman in a professional tournament was achieved by Cecilia Leitch when she won the 1921 Canadian Ladies Open Championship at Rivermead, Ottawa, Canada. In the finals of the match play format, she was declared the winner after being 17 up with only 15 holes to play.

Tony Lema

THE ONLY PROFESSIONAL GOLFER to fall off a cliff.

"Champagne" Tony Lema was known for his high life-style, but a celebration at the 1957 Bing Crosby National Pro-Am at Pebble Beach, California, brought him down to earth. At the 9th hole, Lema hit a great shot and jumped for joy. Unfortunately, he was standing near the edge of a cliff and fell down a steep embankment. Luckily, he escaped with only bumps and bruises.

A. J. Lewis

THE ONLY GOLFER to use 156 putts on a hole.

The ultimate case of the yips belongs to A. J. Lewis. In 1890 he putted 156 times on a single hole at a golf course in Peacehaven, Sussex, England. No matter what he tried, he could not make the ball go into the hole. Frustrated and exhausted, he picked up his ball and went to the next hole without ever holing out.

Harold and Ginny Leyes

THE ONLY HUSBAND AND WIFE GOLFERS to hit holes-in-one on the same hole in the same day.

Ginny Leyes used a driver to ace the 9th hole at the Morris Park Golf Club Course in South Bend, Indiana, on July 21, 1966. One hour later her husband Harold aced the same hole using a 3-iron.

Nils Lied

THE ONLY GOLFER to drive a golf ball 2,640 yards.

Nils Lied, an Australian meteorologist, took advantage of extraordinary weather conditions to drive a golf ball 2,640 yards, a distance of 1-1/2 miles. He drove the ball on a sheet of ice at Mawson Base, Antarctica, in 1962. By the time the ball stopped rolling on the smooth, slick surface, it had traveled about 10 times the length of a drive by an average professional.

Lawson Little

THE ONLY GOLFER to have a ball carried away by a cat.

Lawson Little was a champion golfer who won the 1940 US Open. On May 4, 1934, he suffered a golfing catastrophe. After he hit the ball on the green at the 17th hole at St. Andrews in Scotland, a Persian cat picked it up and ran away. Little was permitted to respot the ball on the green.

Sally Little

THE ONLY GOLFER to shoot a round of 65 in the US Women's Open.

The lowest round in US Women's Open history was a 65 by Sally Little in 1978. The 1978 US Women's Open, played at the Indianapolis Country Club in Indiana, was won, however, by Hollis Stacy. Ironically, the US Open is the only major tournament Little has never won. She won the LPGA Championship in 1980, the Nabisco Dinah Shore in 1982, and the du Maurier Classic in 1988.

A. D. Locke

THE ONLY GOLFER to lose a ball in the flag.

On July 16, 1936, A. D. Locke was playing the 12th hole at the Irish Open at the Royal Dublin Course in Dublin, Ireland. The South African hit a shot right at the pin but lost sight of the ball. When he reached the green, he could not find his ball. He decided to remove the stick to see if the ball had gone in the hole. The ball had lodged in the flag and fell out when he removed the stick. Locke made the short putt for a birdie 2 on the par-3 hole.

Bobby Locke

THE ONLY PROFESSIONAL GOLFER to sleep with his putter.

Bobby Locke was one of the greatest putters in golf history. Locke used his smooth putting stroke to win four British Open titles in 1949, 1950, 1952, and 1957. He loved his putter so much that he actually slept with it.

Nancy Lopez

THE ONLY GOLFER to shoot 268 during a four-round LPGA tournament.

During the 1985 Henredon Classic at High Point, North Carolina, Nancy Lopez set an LPGA tournament record when she won the four-day event with a score of 268. She was a model of consistency, shooting rounds of 66, 67, 69, and 66. Lopez holds many records on the LPGA tour, including being the only player to win five consecutive tournaments.

Joe Lucius

THE ONLY GOLFER to score 13 holes-in-one on the same hole.

On May 12, 1984, Joe Lucius scored his 13th hole-in-one on the 141-yard 15th hole at the Mohawk Golf Club in Tiffin, Ohio. Lucius was nearly as successful on the 10th hole, which he aced 10 times.

Arthur Lynskey

THE ONLY GOLFER to drive a golf ball more than 2 miles.

On June 28, 1968, Arthur Lynskey drove a golf ball off 14,110-foot-high Pikes Peak in Colorado. Lynskey drove the ball 200 yards out and more than 2 miles down.

Bayly MacArthur

THE ONLY GOLFER to hit a ball into a quick-sand trap.

No golfer likes to hit a ball into a sand trap but a sand trap nearly cost Bayly MacArthur his life. In 1931 MacArthur was playing in a tournament in New South Wales, Australia, when he hit a ball into a sand trap. As he stepped into the bunker, he discovered that the sand trap was actually quicksand. His head was about to go under when other golfers managed to pull him to safety.

Johnny McDermott

THE ONLY GOLFER to win the US Open at age 19.

Johnny McDermott was only 19 years old when he won the 1911 US Open, played at the Chicago Golf Club. McDermott proved his victory was not a fluke by repeating as champion the following year.

Charles Macdonald

THE ONLY GOLFER to win the US Amateur by 12 shots.

The first US Amateur competition was also the most lopsided. In 1895 Charles Macdonald defeated Charles Sands 12 and 11 to become the first US Amateur champion. The tournament was played at the Newport Country Club in Rhode Island.

Michael McEvoy

THE ONLY GOLFER to hit a ball into a donkey's ear.

Michael McEvoy once hit a golf ball into a donkey's ear. The incident happened in 1922 at the third hole of the Middleton Golf Course in Cork, Ireland. McEvoy's drive struck a donkey grazing in the fairway and stuck in his ear. The frightened animal ran into the woods. McEvoy found his ball in the woods and scored a double bogey 6 on the hole.

John McMullin

THE ONLY PROFESSIONAL GOLFER to be disqualified twice in the same tournament.

John McMullin's misunderstanding of
the rules caused him to be disqualified
twice in the 1960 Motor City Open in De-
troit, Michigan. On the seventh hole, he
was penalized for taking a practice swing in
a sand trap. Seven holes later, he received
another penalty for striking a moving ball.
He added one penalty shot for each infraction. After he signed his scorecard, he
learned that he was assessed a two-shot
penalty on each hole. As a result McMullin
was disqualified for entering the incorrect
score on two different holes.

Margaret McNeil

THE ONLY GOLFER to win a match by hitting her opponent with a club.

Margaret McNeil and Earlena Adams played for the 1980 Boone Golf Club Championship in North Carolina. The match was headed for a sudden-death play-off when McNeil took a practice swing. On her backswing, she accidentally struck Adams with the club. The blow broke Adams's arm and McNeil was declared the winner.

Lloyd Mangrum

THE ONLY GOLFER to lose the US Open because of a gnat.

Lloyd Mangrum was on his way to winning the 1950 US Open at the Merion Golf Course in Ardmore, Pennsylvania, when he let a gnat bug him. He was about to putt when a gnat landed on his ball. He picked up the ball to remove the gnat and was informed that lifting the ball was an infraction of the rules, which would cost him a two-shot penalty. The penalty cost Mangrum the title as he lost an 18-hole play-off to Ben Hogan.

Norman Manley

THE ONLY GOLFER to score back-to-back albatrosses.

The albatross is the rarest shot in golf. An albatross, or double eagle, is a hole played in 3 under par. Most albatrosses occur on par-5 holes. Norman Manley did it the hard way by scoring holes-in-one on consecutive par-4 holes. The double albatross took place on the seventh and eighth holes of the Del Valle Country Club course in Saugus, California, on September 2, 1964. During his career Manley had over 50 holes-in-one to his credit.

Eddie Martin

THE ONLY CADDIE to cost a golfer the US Open.

A good caddie can help a player win but Eddie Martin actually cost Byron Nelson a chance to win the 1946 US Open, played at the Canterbury Golf Club in Cleveland, Ohio. Martin accidentally kicked Nelson's ball, resulting in a one-stroke penalty. Nelson finished the tournament tied with Lloyd Mangrum but lost the play-off by one shot.

Arnaud Massy

THE ONLY GOLFER from France to win the British Open.

In the long history of the British Open, only one French golfer has won the championship. Arnaud Massy won the French Open in 1906 and added the British Open title the following year. He won three more French Opens, in 1907, 1911, and 1925.

Thomas M'Auliffe

THE ONLY ARMLESS GOLFER to shoot a round of 108.

Although Thomas M'Auliffe was armless, he managed to play golf by holding the club between his right shoulder and cheek. Once at the Buffalo Country Links in New York, he shot a remarkable 108, averaging six shots per hole.

Mrs. J. F. Meehan

THE ONLY TOURNAMENT GOLFER to shoot 161 on a single hole.

Mrs. J. F. Meehan was playing in the 1913 Shawnee Invitational For Ladies at Shawnee-on-Delaware, Pennsylvania, when disaster struck on the 126-yard, par-3, 16th hole. Her golf ball landed in the Binniekill River and began floating downriver. Instead of taking a penalty shot, she decided to chase the ball. She commandeered a boat and caught up with the ball 1½ miles downstream. It took her 40 shots just to beach the ball, then over 100 shots to hack it through the dense forest surrounding the green.

Cary Middlecoff

THE ONLY GOLFER to lose a tournament because he hit a ball into a spectator's pocket.

Cary Middlecoff was an outstanding golfer, winning the US Open in 1949 and 1956 and the Masters in 1955. Middlecoff was leading the 1952 Palm Beach Round Robin tournament when he teed off at the 16th hole of the Wykagyl Country Club course in New Rochelle, New York. His tee shot bounced into the pocket of a spectator standing near the green. The spectator unexpectedly threw the ball into the rough and ran away. Middlecoff scored a double bogey 5 and lost the tournament.

Johnny Miller

THE ONLY GOLFER to shoot 63 in the final round of the US Open.

The most dramatic closing round in US Open history was turned in by Johnny Miller in 1973. Miller fired a tournament record 63 in the closing round of the US Open at Oakmont, Pennsylvania, for a thrilling come-from-behind victory.

Robert Mitera

THE ONLY GOLFER to hit a hole-in-one on a hole of more than 440 yards.

Robert Mitera holds the record for the longest hole-in-one on a straight hole. On October 7, 1965, the 21-year-old golfer was playing the 10th hole of the appropriately named Miracle Hills Golf Club in Omaha, Nebraska. Assisted by a 50-mile-per-hour tail wind and a 290-yard drop-off, Mitera hit a miraculous shot that landed in the cup 447 yards away.

T. J. Moore

THE ONLY GOLFER to hit 20 straight shots
in the water during a tournament.

T. J. Moore achieved golfing immortality
when he hit 20 consecutive balls in the
water on the 18th hole of the Port Arthur
Country Club course in Port Arthur, Texas,
during the 1978 Dryden Invitational. By
the time he reached dry land, Moore had
accumulated 45 strokes on the hole.

John Morgan

THE ONLY GOLFER to be bitten by a rat during the British Open.

During the 1968 British Open at Carnoustie, John Morgan was bitten by a rat. He was on the 10th fairway, about to hit a shot, when a rat ran out of the bushes and bit him. Morgan suffered only a minor wound and was able to continue.

Wanda Morgan

THE ONLY WOMAN GOLFER to shoot a round of 60 over a regulation 18-hole course.

On July 11, 1929, teenager Wanda Morgan shot the lowest 18-hole score by a woman when she needed only 60 strokes to complete the Westgate and Birchington Golf Course in Kent, England. She played the front 9 in 31, then blistered the back 9 in 29.

David Morris

THE ONLY GOLFER to hit 1,290 drives in one hour.

David Morris hit 1,290 practice drives in one hour on May 21, 1988, at the Abergele Golf Club Course in Clwyd, Wales. Morris averaged a drive every three seconds during the practice session.

Old Tom Morris

THE ONLY GOLFER to win the British Open at age 46.

Old Tom Morris dominated the early years of the British Open. In 1867 he won his fourth British Open played in Prestwick, Scotland, at the age of 46. His son, Tom Morris, Jr., also won four British Opens before his untimely death at the age of 25.

Tom Morris, Jr.

THE ONLY GOLFER to win the British Open at age 17.

Seventeen-year-old Tom Morris, Jr., became the youngest player ever to win the British Open when he won the 1868 tournament held at Prestwick, Ayrshire, Scotland. To prove it was not a fluke, he became the only player to win the British Open four consecutive times. His father, known as Old Tom Morris, also won four British Opens, making them the most successful father-son golfers in history.

Tommy Nakajima

THE ONLY GOLFER to shoot 13 on the 13th hole during the Masters.

The 475-yard 13th hole at Augusta National Golf Course is one of the most challenging in the world. During the 1978 Masters, Japanese golfer Tommy Nakajima found out how difficult the 13th at Augusta can be. He was assessed five penalty shots for hitting a ball into Rae's Creek, grounding a club in the hazard, and having a ball strike his foot. Nakajima carded a 13 for the par 5 hole, the most disastrous score for a hole in Masters history.

Byron Nelson

THE ONLY PROFESSIONAL GOLFER to win 11 tournaments in a row.

In 1945 Byron Nelson experienced the greatest year in golf history when he won a record 19 tournaments on the professional tour. One record almost certain to stand forever was his amazing feat of winning 11 consecutive tournaments. The streak began on March 11, when he won the Miami Fourball, and ended on August 4, with a victory in the Canadian Open. His total earnings for the 11 tournaments was $30,250. A similar streak by a golfer today would be worth nearly $2 million.

Jack Newton

THE ONLY PROFESSIONAL GOLFER to flee a hole because he had ants in his pants.

Jack Newton was leading the Cock o' the North Tournament in Ndola, Zambia, when he arrived at the 17th hole. He was not aware that the Ndola Golf Course was inhabited by ferocious African ants. When he hit a shot too near one of their nests, he was attacked by hundreds of ants, which ran up his leg. After being bitten several times, Newton tore off his clothes and fled the hole. Once order was restored, the Australian regained his composure and won the tournament.

Jack Nicklaus

THE ONLY GOLFER to win 20 major tournament titles.

Jack Nicklaus is considered by many experts to be the greatest golfer who ever lived. Perhaps the most remarkable feat in golf history is his record of 20 major tournament victories. The Golden Bear has won six Masters, five PGAs, four US Opens, three British Opens, and two US Amateur titles. In 1986, the 46-year-old Nicklaus became the oldest player to win the Masters.

Christy O'Connor, Jr.

THE ONLY GOLFER to shoot seven consecutive birdies in the British Open.

In the first round of the 1985 British
Open, Christy O'Connor, Jr., shot seven
consecutive birdies en route to a round of
64. He birdied holes 4 through 10 at the
Sandwich, England, course. O'Connor
finished third in the Open behind winner
Sandy Lyle.

Porky Oliver

THE ONLY GOLFER to lose the US Open for teeing off too early.

Porky Oliver was poised to win his first US Open. He was so eager to play the final round of the 1940 Open at the Canterbury Golf Club in Cleveland, Ohio, that he teed off a half hour too soon. He finished the tournament tied for the lead with Lawson Little and Byron Nelson but was disqualified for teeing off too early. The play-off was won by Lawson Little.

Francis Ouimet

THE ONLY CADDIE to win the US Open.

Amateur Francis Ouimet shocked the golf world in 1913 when he won the US Open. Ouimet was a caddie who only entered the Open because the site of the tournament, the Brookline Golf Course in Brookline, Massachusetts, was across the street from his house. Ouimet defeated the great English golfers Harry Vardon and Ted Ray in a play-off.

Arnold Palmer

THE ONLY GOLFER on the Senior Tour to score holes-in-one on consecutive days.

In 1986 Arnold Palmer became the only golfer on the Senior Tour to make holes-in-one on consecutive days. Palmer's feat took place at the Senior PGA Tour Chrysler Cup played at the TPC Avenel Course near Washington, DC. He aced the 187-yard third hole each day. The odds against such an occurrence were calculated at 9 million to 1.

Scott Palmer

THE ONLY GOLFER to score 100 holes-in-one.

Scott Palmer of San Diego, California, holds nearly every record for scoring holes-in-one. He is the only golfer to record 100 holes-in-one. During a one-year period between June 1983 and June 1984, Palmer had 33 aces. In October 1983, he had holes-in-one in four consecutive rounds.

John Panton

THE ONLY GOLFER to be disqualified in the British Open for practicing.

John Panton felt he needed some extra practice during the 1946 British Open. In the evening he practiced his putting on the St. Andrews Course. When officials discovered that Panton was practicing on the qualifying course between rounds, they disqualified him.

Willie Park

THE ONLY GOLFER to win the British Open in one day.

The first British Open took place on October 17, 1860, at the Prestwick Golf Club in Prestwick, Scotland. Eight golfers competed in the 36-hole tournament. Three 12-hole rounds were played—all in the same day. The winner was Willie Park with a 36-hole score of 174.

Philip Parkin

THE ONLY GOLFER to be carried piggyback during the British Open.

Philip Parkin injured his leg during the 1985 British Open played at St. George's Golf Course in Sandwich, England. It appeared that he was going to be unable to continue because he could not walk between shots. His playing partner, Nick Faldo, came up with a unique solution. Faldo carried Parkin piggyback, enabling him to finish the round.

Jerry Pate

THE ONLY GOLFER to win a professional tournament by more than 20 strokes.

Jerry Pate was a highly successful golfer on the PGA tour for many years. He is best remembered for jumping into a water hazard to celebrate his victory in the 1982 Tournament Players' Championship at Ponte Vedra Beach in Florida. That same year he set a record for the largest winning margin in a tournament when he won the Colombian Open by an incredible 21 strokes.

Gary Player

THE ONLY PROFESSIONAL GOLFER to be attacked by killer bees.

Gary Player has won 9 major tournaments in his career but he was no match for a swarm of killer bees. In 1966 he was matched against Jack Nicklaus in an exhibition in Zwartkop, South Africa. They were in the middle of the round when they were attacked by killer bees. The two golfers fled to safety and discreetly decided to halve the hole rather than replay it.

Don Pooley

THE ONLY GOLFER to win $1 million for a hole-in-one.

A million dollar bonus was offered for any golfer scoring a hole-in-one on the 17th hole of the 1987 Hertz Bay Hill Classic in Orlando, Florida. Don Pooley collected the bonus by scoring a hole-in-one, earning more prize money with one shot than he had won during his professional career.

Philippe Porquier

THE ONLY GOLFER to shoot a 20 on a hole in the French Open.

During the 1978 French Open in La Baule, France, Philippe Porquier set a new record for futility. On the 13th hole at La Baule Golf Course, rated par 5, he shot a 20, the worst one-hole score in the history of the European tour.

Douglas Porteous

THE ONLY GOLFER to score four holes-in-one over a 39-hole span.

Douglas Porteous is the only golfer to score four holes-in-one in less than three complete rounds. On September 26, 1974, Porteous aced the third and sixth holes at the Ruchill Golf Course in Glasgow, Scotland. Two days later, he aced the fifth hole at Ruchill and on September 30 scored a hole-in-one on the sixth hole at the Clydebank and District Golf Course in Glasgow. During his streak he averaged a hole-in-one every 10 holes.

Arthur Powell

THE ONLY GOLFER to make a hole-in-one after hitting the ball out of bounds.

Arthur Powell of Cork, Ireland, hit a terrible drive on a 265-yard hole. The ball sliced out of bounds and hit the roof of a house. Powell watched in amazement as the ball bounced back onto the green and rolled into the cup for a hole-in-one.

Nick Price

THE ONLY GOLFER to shoot 63 during a round of the Masters.

Nick Price of Zimbabwe set the record for the lowest round in Masters history when he shot a 63 during the 1986 tournament. The Masters is held every April at the beautiful Augusta National Golf Course in Georgia. Despite Price's brilliant round, the tournament was won by 46-year-old Jack Nicklaus, his sixth Masters title.

Jackie Pung

THE ONLY GOLFER to lose the US Women's Open for signing an incorrect scorecard.

An incorrect scorecard cost Jackie Pung her chance to win the US Women's Open. At the end of 72 holes, she was tied with Betsy Rawls. She was unaware that her playing partner, Betty Jameson, had marked the wrong score on her card for the fourth hole. When Pung signed the card, she was automatically disqualified. Ironically, at the same tournament, Pung also made a scoring error that resulted in Jameson's disqualification.

Alain Reisco

THE ONLY GOLFER to play three rounds of golf on three continents in one day.

Airline executive Alain Reisco decided he wanted to play three rounds of golf on three different continents within a 24-hour period. He was joined by fellow executives Sherl Folger, Marvin Fritz, and Art Sues. The foursome teed off at 5 A.M. at the Royal Mohammedia Course in Casablanca, Morocco. At 1:30 P.M. they played the Torrequebrada Golf Course in Málaga, Spain. By 6:30 P.M. they were teeing off at the North Hills Country Club in Manhasset, New York.

Alice Ritzman

THE ONLY WOMAN GOLFER to have three eagles in one round.

Alice Ritzman is the only professional golfer in the history of the LPGA tour to score three eagles in one round. Ritzman's three-eagle performance occurred in the second round of the 1979 Colgate European Open.

Isabella Robertson

THE ONLY WOMAN GOLFER to win a tournament at age 50.

The oldest woman golfer to win a tournament was Isabella Robertson. She was 50 years old when she won the 1986 Scottish Women's Championship.

Marie Robie

THE ONLY WOMAN GOLFER to score a hole-in-one on a 393-yard hole.

Marie Robie of Wollaston, Massachusetts, was playing the 393-yard first hole of the Furnace Brook Golf Club in Wollaston on September 4, 1949, when the unexpected happened. Hoping to hit a long drive to set up a birdie on the par-4 hole, she hit the shot of her life, the longest hole-in-one ever recorded by a woman.

Phil Rodgers

THE ONLY GOLFER to lose the US Open because he hit four shots out of a tree.

Phil Rodgers was on the leader board of the 1962 US Open when he hit his tee shot on the 17th hole at the Oakmont Country Club course in Pennsylvania. His shot landed high in a pine tree. Rodgers climbed the tree in an attempt to avoid a penalty shot. It took him four strokes to chip the ball out of the tree, resulting in a quadruple bogey 8 on the par-4 hole. The hole proved costly as Rodgers lost the tournament by two strokes.

Floyd Rood

THE ONLY GOLFER to use the entire United States as a golf course.

In October 1964, Rood became the only golfer to hit a golf ball from the Pacific coast to the Atlantic coast of the United States. It took him 114,737 strokes and 13 months to complete the 3,397-mile journey. Along the way Rood lost 3,511 golf balls.

Erna Ross

THE ONLY WOMAN GOLFER to score a hole-in-one at age 95.

The oldest woman golfer to score a hole-in-one was 95-year-old Erna Ross. On May 25, 1986, she aced the 112-yard 17th hole at the Everglades Golf Club in Palm Beach, Florida.

Paul Runyan

THE ONLY GOLFER to win the PGA Championship by eight shots.

Paul Runyan won his second PGA Championship in 1938. In those days the tournament was conducted in a match play format. Runyan defeated Sam Snead 8 and 7 in the championship match, the largest margin of victory in PGA history. The tournament was played at the Shawnee Country Club in Shawnee-on-Delaware, Pennsylvania.

George Russell

THE ONLY GOLFER to hit a drive 300 yards backwards.

At the 1913 Braids Tournament in Scotland, George Russell hit a 300-yard drive. The only problem was that the ball traveled backwards. On the backswing, his club struck the ball, which rolled down a steep hill behind the tee. By the time the ball stopped rolling, it was 300 yards from the elevated tee.

Doug Sanders

THE ONLY PROFESSIONAL GOLFER to be disqualified for signing too many autographs.

Popular Doug Sanders led the 1966 Pensacola Open in Florida by four shots after shooting a 67 in the second round. He was mobbed by his fans and graciously signed dozens of autographs. The only thing he didn't sign was his scorecard and he was disqualified. The tournament was won by Gay Brewer.

Charles Sands

THE ONLY AMERICAN MALE GOLFER to win an Olympic gold medal.

Charles Sands of the United States won the first Olympic gold medal in men's golf at the 1900 Paris Olympics. He shot 167 in the 36-hole competition to defeat Walter Rutherford of Great Britain by one shot.

Gene Sarazen

THE ONLY GOLFER to score a hole-in-one during the British Open at age 71.

Gene Sarazen's amazing career spanned over a half century. In 1922, at the age of 20, he won the US Open and became the youngest PGA winner in history. In 1935 he made the famous double eagle on the 15th hole at the Augusta National, which led to his first Masters title. In 1973 he capped off his long career by becoming the oldest player ever to score a hole-in-one during the British Open. The ace came on the famed Postage Stamp Hole—so known because of the tiny size of the green—at Troon in Scotland.

Patty Sheehan

THE ONLY GOLFER to win the LPGA Tournament by 10 shots.

Patty Sheehan set a record when she won the 1984 LPGA Tournament by 10 shots at the Jack Nicklaus Sports Center in Kings Island, Ohio. It was the second consecutive year that Sheehan won the prestigious tournament.

Alan Shepard

THE ONLY GOLFER to hit a 6-iron on the moon.

Alan Shepard was America's first man in space. In 1971 he was a member of the Apollo 14 crew on a mission to the moon. To demonstrate the moon's reduced gravity, Shepard became the first golfer on the lunar surface. He hit a 6-iron shot that, he said, "went for miles and miles."

Curtis Sifford

THE ONLY PROFESSIONAL GOLFER to have a shot land in a hot dog.

During the Quad Cities Open in Iowa. Curtis Sifford sliced a shot into the crowd. The ball landed in a hot dog dropped by a spectator. Sifford removed the mustard from his ball and proceeded to hit his next shot onto the green.

Alfred Smith

THE ONLY GOLFER to shoot 55 on a regulation 18-hole course.

Alfred Smith made golfing history when he shot a 55 over an 18-hole course at Woolacombe, England, on January 1, 1936. The 15-under-par round by the English professional was two shots better than the existing 18-hole record.

Ernest Smith

THE ONLY GOLFER to play golf in five countries in one day.

On June 12, 1939, Ernest Smith played golf in five countries in one day. He played rounds in Scotland, Ireland, the Isle of Man, England, and Wales. Despite playing five rounds in one day, his scores were exceptional: 70, 76, 76, 72, and 68.

Paul Smith

THE ONLY GOLF SPONSOR to offer a prepaid funeral as a prize for a hole-in-one.

The 1985 New South Wales Open in Canberra, Australia, offered an unusual prize for a hole-in-one. Anyone hitting a hole-in-one on the eighth hole would win a prepaid funeral, offered by one of the tournament sponsors, funeral director Paul Smith. If a sudden-death play-off had been necessary, it would have started on the eighth hole.

J. C. Snead

THE ONLY PROFESSIONAL GOLFER to putt with his hat.

For years J. C. Snead's panama hat had been his trademark, but during the 1977 Tournament Players Championship it proved to be his downfall. He had just hit a shot on the fourth hole at the Sawgrass Golf Course in Ponte Vedra Beach, Florida, when a 50-mile-per-hour gust blew off his hat. His hat traveled straight down the fairway and struck his ball, which was over 100 feet away on the green. PGA officials penalized Snead two shots because he had "putted" with his hat.

Sam Snead

THE ONLY GOLFER to lose a tournament because he hit a shot into the men's bathroom.

Sam Snead won a record 84 tour victories during his long and distinguished career. He was the oldest player, at age 52, to win a US tour victory. Snead also holds the dubious distinction of being the only player to lose a tournament by hitting a ball into the men's bathroom. Snead was playing in the Cleveland Open in Cleveland, Ohio, when an errant shot sailed through the open door of the men's locker room. The ball ricocheted into the men's bathroom. Snead incurred a two-shot penalty and lost the tournament by one stroke.

Harold Snider

THE ONLY GOLFER to score three holes-in-one during a round of golf at age 75.

Few golfers have scored three holes-in-one in a lifetime but 75-year-old Harold Snider had three in one round of golf. The triple aces occurred on the 8th, 13th, and 14th holes of the Ironwood Golf Course in Phoenix, Arizona, on June 9, 1976.

Angelo Spagnola

THE ONLY GOLFER to shoot a round of 257.

In 1985 *Golf Digest* organized a tournament to find the worst avid golfer in the
United States. The winner was Angelo
Spagnola of Fayette City, Pennsylvania,
who shot a mind-boggling 257 for 18 holes.
He capped off his record-breaking round
with a 66 on the 17th hole.

Lefty Stackhouse

THE ONLY PROFESSIONAL GOLFER to punch himself out.

Lefty Stackhouse was a professional golfer who was his own worst enemy. After hitting a bad shot, he often hit his hand or whatever part of his body he felt had made the mistake. One time, after missing a crucial putt, he punched himself so hard that he knocked himself out.

Craig Stadler

THE ONLY PROFESSIONAL GOLFER to be disqualified for using a towel.

On the 14th hole of the Torrey Pines Golf Course in La Jolla, California, during the third round of the 1987 Andy Williams Open, Craig Stadler hit a ball beneath some pine trees. He placed a towel on the muddy ground so he could kneel to hit the next shot. Stadler finished second in the tournament only to discover that he had been disqualified for signing an incorrect scorecard. The officials had assessed him a two-stroke penalty for improving his stance by use of the towel. Since he did not add the penalty to his score at the time, he was disqualified.

Scott Statler

THE ONLY GOLFER to score a hole-in-one at age four.

Scott Statler was the youngest golfer ever to score a hole-in-one. He was only four years old when he aced the seventh hole at the Statler's Par 3 Golf Course in Greensburg, Pennsylvania, on July 30, 1962.

Jimmy Stewart

THE ONLY GOLFER to be attacked by a cobra during a tournament.

Jimmy Stewart (not the actor) was about to hit a shot during the 1972 Singapore Open when he was attacked by a 10-foot cobra, which apparently had mistaken the golf ball for an egg. Stewart used his club to kill the snake but was startled to see another snake slither from the cobra's mouth. He used the iron to dispatch the second snake.

Payne Stewart

THE ONLY PROFESSIONAL GOLFER to lose his knickers on a bet.

Former PGA champion Payne Stewart is immediately recognizable on the golf course because of his distinctive knickers. Before playing an exhibition match in 1988 at the Hercules Country Club in Wilmington, Delaware, he made a wager he lived to regret. He bet three women professionals that he could beat their best ball. If he lost he would remove his knickers; if they lost they would have to take off their shorts. On the final hole he lost the bet and, to the delight of the spectators, removed his knickers.

Charles Stock

THE ONLY GOLFER to play 44 rounds in one day.

When someone sees Charles Stock on the golf course, they usually let him play through. Stock laid claim to the title of the world's fastest golfer when he played 783 holes at the Arcadia Country Club in Lyndhurst, Ohio, on July 20, 1987. Using an electric golf cart for transportation, he nearly averaged a round of golf every half hour.

Hal Sutton

THE ONLY GOLFER to shoot a 36-hole score of 131 in the PGA Championship.

Hal Sutton shot the best back-to-back rounds in PGA history on the way to winning the 1983 championship. He shot rounds of 65 and 66 for a 36-hole total of 131.

Robert Taylor

THE ONLY GOLFER to ace the same hole on three successive days.

The 16th hole at the Hunstanton Golf Course in Norfolk, England, was clearly a favorite of Robert Taylor. Beginning on May 31, 1974, he aced the 188-yard hole on three successive days.

Arthur Thompson

THE ONLY GOLFER to shoot a round of 103 at age 103.

In 1973 Arthur Thompson became the oldest golfer to shoot his age. The 103-year-old shot a round of 103 at the Uplands Golf Course in British Columbia, Canada.

Randolph Timmerman

THE ONLY GOLFER to throw a golf club 61 yards.

Randolph Timmerman holds the record for the longest toss of a golf club, and he wasn't even angry. He was a participant in the 1936 Club Throwing Tournament at the Druid Hills Country Club in Atlanta, Georgia. His throw of 61 yards was an all-time record.

The Toogoods

THE ONLY GOLFERS in the same family to finish first, second, and third in a tournament.

The Toogood family proved to be too good for the competition at the 1956 Tasmanian Open in Tasmania. Peter Toogood finished first; his father Alfred finished second; and his brother John finished third.

Lee Trevino

THE ONLY GOLFER to win three national championships in three weeks.

No golfer has ever experienced a better three-week period than Lee Trevino did in 1971. Trevino won the US Open, Canadian Open, and British Open in successive weeks.

Leonard Tupling

THE ONLY GOLFER to shoot 29 under par during a 72-hole tournament.

British golfer Leonard Tupling won the 1981 Nigerian Open, shooting a world record 29-under-par 255 for the 72-hole tournament. Tupling shot rounds of 63, 66, 62, and 64 over the Ikoyi Golf Club Course in Lagos, Nigeria.

Mike Turnesa

THE ONLY GOLFER to have six sons become professional golfers.

Mike Turnesa of Elmsford, New York, dreamed of having his sons become professional golfers. Six of his sons did become professional golfers and son Jim won the 1952 PGA Championship. The only son who did not turn professional was Willie, who remained an amateur and won the US Amateur Championship in 1938 and 1948.

Harry Vardon

THE ONLY GOLFER to win six British Open championships.

Englishman Harry Vardon is the only player to win six British Open titles. Often called "the father of modern golf," Vardon won the tournament in 1896, 1898, 1899, 1903, 1911, and 1914. He was 44 years old when he won his last British Open title, in Prestwick, England.

Cyril Walker

THE ONLY PROFESSIONAL GOLFER to be
arrested for slow play.

Cyril Walker, the 1924 US Open winner,
was the most deliberate player in golf history. He was repeatedly warned for slow
play. The problem climaxed at the 1930
Los Angeles Open played at the Riviera
Country Club. Walker was disqualified on
the ninth hole for slow play. When he re-
fused to leave the course, the Englishman
was dragged away, kicking and screaming,
by Los Angeles police.

Art Wall

THE ONLY PROFESSIONAL GOLFER to shoot 42 holes-in-one during his career.

Art Wall had a long and successful career on the PGA tour. Between 1936 and 1979 he scored 42 holes-in-one, more than any other professional golfer, averaging nearly one a year.

Charles Ward

THE ONLY GOLFER to score two holes-in-one at the British Open.

Charles Ward is the only player to shoot two holes-in-one in the British Open. He aced the eighth hole at St. Andrews Course in the 1946 Open. Two years later he shot another hole-in-one on the 13th hole at Muirfield.

Jo Ann Washam

THE ONLY GOLFER to shoot two holes-in-one in an LPGA tournament.

In the second round of the 1979 Women's Kemper Open at the Mesa Verde Country Club in Colorado, Jo Ann Washam aced the 16th hole. She aced the 17th hole during the final round to become the only woman in LPGA tour history to score two holes-in-one in the same tournament.

Al Watrous

THE ONLY GOLFER to blow a 9-hole lead with 12 holes to play in the PGA Championship.

American Al Watrous appeared on his way to an easy victory in the 1932 PGA Championship. He led Bobby Cruickshank by 9-holes with 12 holes to play in the championship match at the Keller Golf Course in St. Paul, Minnesota. Cruickshank shot a 30 on the back 9 and defeated Watrous in a play-off.

Tom Watson

THE ONLY GOLFER to win the British Open on five different courses.

Tom Watson has won the British Open five times—each time on a different golf course. He has won at Carnoustie (1975), Turnberry (1977), Muirfield (1980), Troon (1982), and Birkdale (1983).

George Wegener

THE ONLY GOLFER to score a hole-in-one in one country after teeing off in another.

The Gateway Golf Course is located on the border of the United States and Canada. Fourteen-year-old George Wegener of Portal, North Dakota, teed off on the ninth hole in Canada and scored a hole-in-one on the ninth green in the United States.

Tom Weiskopf

THE ONLY GOLFER to hit five consecutive shots in the water at the Masters.

Tom Weiskopf finished second in the Masters four times but he does hold one Masters record he would rather do without. The 12th hole at the Augusta National in Augusta, Georgia, is one of the toughest par-3 holes in the world. Weiskopf showed how difficult it can be by hitting five straight tee shots into Rae's Creek during the 1980 Masters. He took a 13 on the hole.

Jack Westland

THE ONLY GOLFER over age 47 to win the US Amateur Championship.

Jack Westland is the oldest golfer to win the US Amateur Championship. He was 47 years, 8 months, and 9 days old when he won the title in 1952.

A. Whedden

THE ONLY GOLFER to be assisted by a lamb.

In 1928 a golfer identified as A. Whedden played a round of golf at the Burton-on-Trent Golf Club Course in England. He hit the ball safely on the green. As he walked toward the green, a lamb grabbed his ball and dropped it in the cup.

Kathy Whitworth

THE ONLY GOLFER to win 88 tournaments in the United States.

Kathy Whitworth won 88 tournaments during her career, which spanned from 1962 to 1985. The 88 victories not only established an LPGA record but also were four more than the men's PGA record set by the legendary Sam Snead.

G. S. Williams, Jr.

THE ONLY GOLFER to hit a drive 22,834 feet above sea level.

G. S. Williams, Jr., took golf to new heights when he hit a golf ball from the top of Aconcagua Mountain in Argentina on January 22, 1989. The peak is 22,834 feet (more than 4 miles) above sea level.

Mickey Wright

THE ONLY GOLFER to win 13 LPGA tournaments in one year.

Thirteen was a lucky number for Mickey Wright. In 1963 she won 13 tournaments on the LPGA tour, a record that still stands. She dominated women's golf between 1958 and 1964, winning four US Women's Opens and four US Ladies PGA titles during that period. Wright retired in 1978 with 82 career titles.

Colin Young

THE ONLY GOLFER to play 70 rounds of golf in a week.

In July 1989, Colin Young of Pattingham, England, played 70 rounds of golf in one week at the Patshull Park Golf Club in Pattingham. This translates to 180 holes of golf per day, or 7½ holes per hour.

Babe Zaharias

THE ONLY GOLFER to win the US Women's Open by 12 shots.

Babe Didrikson Zaharias was perhaps the greatest all-around female athlete. At the 1932 Summer Olympics in Los Angeles, the 18-year-old won gold medals in the high jump, javelin, and 80-meter hurdles. During the 1940s she became one of the top professional women golfers, once winning 14 consecutive tournaments. In 1953 it appeared her career was over when she underwent an operation for cancer. The following year she staged an amazing comeback, winning the US Women's Open by a record 12 shots.

Mary Beth Zimmerman

THE ONLY GOLFER to shoot 8 straight birdies in an LPGA tournament.

Mary Beth Zimmerman got her name into the record books at the 1984 Illinois Rail Charity Classic. She made eight consecutive birdies while shooting a 28 on the back 9 of a round of 64.

FLOYD CONNER is the co-author of Day-by-Day in Cincinnati Reds History, Day-by-Day in Cincinnati Bengals History, and This Date in Sports History, as well as the author of numerous articles about golf and other sports. He lives with his wife, Susan, and their son, Travis, in Cincinnati.